THIS WALKER BOOK BELONGS TO:

_____

_____

_____

_____

For Louisa

First published 1986 by Walker Books Ltd
87 Vauxhall Walk, London SE11 5HJ

This edition published 2005 for Index Books Ltd

2 4 6 8 10 9 7 5 3 1

© 1986 Shirley Hughes

The right of Shirley Hughes to be identified as author/illustrator of this work
has been asserted by her in accordance with the Copyright, Designs and Patents Act 1988

This book has been typeset in Vendome

Printed in China

British Library Cataloguing in Publication Data: a catalogue record for this book
is available from the British Library

ISBN 0-7445-6982-6

www.walkerbooks.co.uk

All Shapes
and Sizes

Shirley Hughes

WALKER BOOKS
AND SUBSIDIARIES
LONDON · BOSTON · SYDNEY · AUCKLAND

Boxes have flat sides,
Balls are round.

High is far up in the sky,
Low is near the ground.

Some of us are rather short,

Some are tall.

Some pets are large,

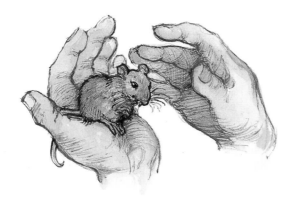

Some are small.

Our cat's very fat,
Next door's is thin.

Big Teddy's out,
Little Teddy's in.

Squeeze through narrow spaces,

Run through wide,

Climb up the ladder,

Slip down the slide.

Get behind to push,

Get in front to pull.

This

jar's

empty,

Now

it's

full.

Hats can be many sizes,

So can feet,

Children of all ages

playing in the street.

We can stand up very straight,

or we can bend.

Here's a beginning,

and this is the end!

WALKER BOOKS

The Nursery Collection

SHIRLEY HUGHES says that she found working on The Nursery Collection "very stimulating". They were her first books for very young children and she remarks that creating them was "concentrated and exhausting because it was like actually being with a very small child." The brother and sister featured in the books reappear in her book of seasonal verse *Out and About* and in a series of books about "doing words" – *Bouncing*, *Chatting*, *Giving* and *Hiding* – now collected in a single volume as *Let's Join In*.

Shirley Hughes has won numerous awards, including the Kate Greenaway Medal for *Dogger* and the Eleanor Farjeon Award for services to children's literature. In 1999 she was awarded the OBE. Among her many popular books are the *Alfie and Annie Rose*, *Lucy and Tom* and *Tales of Trotter Street* series.

Shirley and her husband, a retired architect, have lived in the same house in west London for more than forty years. They have three grown-up children and six grandchildren.

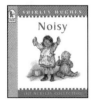

ISBN 0-7445-6983-4 (pb)   ISBN 0-7445-6986-9 (pb)   ISBN 0-7445-6984-2 (pb)   ISBN 0-7445-6981-8 (pb)   ISBN 0-7445-6985-0 (pb)   ISBN 0-7445-6982-6 (pb)